DIVORCE STORIES

STORIES OF DIVORCES WITH MORALS TO LEARN

ZARREEN KHAN

DISCLAIMER

The names taken in the book are fictional and any resemblance to actual persons living or dead is entirely coincidental.

The book is written based on the author's experiences and research done on the subject and reader's view may vary.

This book is not intended to defame or hurt anybody's feeling but is written with a sole purpose to diminish the causes of divorces in our society.

Contents

Acknowledgements *vii*

1. Introduction 1

2. Case 1 8

3. Case 2 12

4. Case 3 21

5. Case 4 34

6. Case 5 44

7. Case 6 48

8. What We Learned 50

9. General Causes Of Divorces 60

10. 9 Golden Mantras 80

Quotes 91

Acknowledgements

I would like to thank my husband Hashim Khan who persuaded me and encouraged me throughout my journey of this book.

I'm immensely grateful to my parents who are the guiding light of my life.

Finally my heartfelt thanks to those whose lives inspired me to write this book.

CHAPTER ONE

INTRODUCTION

Today we're seeing boom in technology, boom in jobs, products, entertainment, vehicles, mobiles and so also boom in divorces.

Gone are the days when we Indians use to discuss about divorces happening in America because now our own country is witnessing it in its highest peak.

According to reports, divorces have doubled over the past two decades with most cases of divorces happening in the urban arrears of India. Whether it's the interference of family, the growing independence of women, awareness of rights or education, there are many factors contributing to this rise. Impulse wedding, adultery, dowry, infertility, impulse divorces also are contributing to this number.

Besides, more awareness of mental health and the importance of leading a fulfilling and happy life among the young are bringing about this change in the whole institution of marriage. Now even parents are extending the much needed support to their children willing to go through an arduous process of divorce, making happiness paramount, something which was unlikely few years back.

India is officially considered to have one of the lowest divorce rates in the world i.e., 1%. This is immeasurably small when compared to the average statistics for the United States which is 45%.

You may feel quite ecstatic looking at the figures but does it really shows the real face of our marriages?

According to family attorney Vasudha N R, though we may have the lowest rate in the world, we definitely have a large number of unhappy marriages. The stigma attached to the definition of divorce is one of the biggest reasons people continue them.

The institution of marriage in India is not just a holy but an expensive and grand affair. It's a system in which more than half of Indian values and traditions are intertwined. Marriage is the most sacred and pure form of Indian custom, the breaking up of which is considered to be a great ordeal. The end of marriage is especially traumatic for women and her family due to the deep rooted patriarchy that largely governs Indian society even today.

It isn't that difficult to come to the realization that many people have suffered for their lifetime under abusive marriages just for the sake of escaping the tormenting life that divorce brings itself. Those few who actually go through with a divorce face unimaginable treatment from family, friends and extended relatives. The taboo of divorces is such that our society normalizes death over it.

Also, one of the main reasons for such a low percentage is the lack of clear regulations for registering marriages.Many unregistered marriages are still happening in the lower and upper region of our country.

Many marriages are solemnized in holy places like temples, mosques and gurudwara. Though it becomes legal it is not officially registered in the government data unless and until marriage certificates are made through registration offices.

Just like many marriages are not registered so also many divorces are not registered. In many cases husband or wife just leaves their spouses for their own reasons. So though they are not divorced legally or have not have not filed their divorces but actually they are divorced.

It can be seen that no one can give the exact data of broken homes in India, but one thing is sure 10-15 years earlier we hardly use to come across any cases of divorces in our entire social circle but now I myself have witnessed eleven cases of divorces which is a high digit for a person whose social circle does not consist of many people.

Now the question arises why today we are witnessing so many divorces around us?

I have heard many old generation people saying that ----

'We have given too much liberty and freedom to our girls, now that they are earning they don't want to look after their home which is their primary responsibility.'

'Today mothers are not teaching their daughters household chores due to which they fail drastically after marriage.'

'Today's generation has become addicted to their phones due to which they have become too lazy to fulfill their household responsibility.'

'In our times we use to raise ten twelve children single handedly without any support from the husband or in-laws and even use to perform all the household chores without any technology. Now that they are getting so much ease and support still they can't take care of their family.'

'Problem with today's generation is that they expect too much from their marriage and when this expectation is not met problems arises leading to divorce.'

So you see many mouths many reasons.

Are these the real reasons behind unsuccessful marriage or the real reason is much deeper to be dug out?

Why the stigma against divorce is only raised on women?

Why only divorcee woman has to suffer social backlash and exclusion and not man?

Why the allegation of breaking home is put on women?

We have seen many divorcee men get married again easily without any huddle but for women things are tough.

When marriage is about equal partnership, a lifelong contract between both the parties why the burden of keeping the families united is only placed on the woman and her family?

Is it not true that many dowry harassment cases, domestic violence and abuses cases victims are only the women?

So you see it's a long wrangle not easy to be solved. Every party has their own valid arguments and justification. Not every time fault lays in the woman so also not every time faults lies in the man.

Many times mistakes are done from both the ends and many times it is nobody's mistakes but the circumstances.

So it is necessary to look into each and every aspect of the situation.

CHAPTER TWO

CASE 1

Amit and Jyoti were dating each other for 6 years. They both first met each other while doing their post-graduation and from the beginning itself love started blooming between the two. They were mature and also from the same caste so there were no objection from their families as well. After setting up their careers in respective field they decided to marry.

Everything was going as per their plans and even after marriage things were going smoothly between them. No issues no complaints from both the ends. After four years of marriage they planned their first baby. Though their decision was great it became strenuous on both of them. They both were working and as they were living away from their families they didn't get any support from them as well.

After maternity leave Jyoti again joined her company leaving her baby in a daycare near her office. Everything was going well when suddenly after few months they both filed for their divorce in the court. Jyoti even took transfer to some other city and took their baby along with her so that Amit could not meet him.

So now the question arises what went so wrong that their relationship became sour to such an extent. Five years of marriage and eleven years of relation broke down to pieces. Allegations and blame game was done from both the sides but the end result was DIVORCE.

In this case they were living away from their families so there was no direct interference of the in-laws. They knew each other for so many years so no compatibility issues. Neither Amit nor Jyoti were having any illicit affairs outside their marriage. Neither of them had short-temper issues whereas both of them were very soft spoken people. So we see all the general causes of divorces are negated here.

Here Amit and Jyoti started becoming unsatisfied with each other. What they want from their partners they were unable to communicate, either because of lack of time or because of their ego which starts from- why should I tell her/him, can't s/he understand.

Slowly this dissatisfaction leads to frustration and we unconsciously become that grumpy person who gets annoyed or lose their temper on petty issues.

These are the early signs where the partners should take their time out and confront each other about the matter. Confrontation is a process which takes time. First two times they will say 'nothing happened' or 'Everything is fine' then in the third trial they'll blurt out what's bothering them. This is normal human tendency after marriage. So you have to be patient and persistence in your efforts.

Another point to consider is when you plan a baby a woman has to go through lots of things ---

Depression, mood swings, sleepless nights, pain, mental agony, distress, vomiting, not being able to eat, restlessness racking pain and many more during the entire nine months of pregnancy and many months after delivery.

During this time a woman needs and she expect emotional and physical support from her husband. When this expectation is not met then frustration, ill feeling for the other, anguishes' start developing and it weakens the relationship to the core.

Husbands on the other hand not understanding what is going on, sometimes do things that add fuel to the fire. It is imperative in relations to know and understand your partners well. Your relationship should touch that level where you don't have to tell each other what you are feeling, they should understand on their own. To build up till that level requires effort, patience and time which most of the time couple don't invest.

What is investment?

Investment is the dedication of an asset to attain an increase in value over a period of time. It requires a sacrifice of some present asset, such as time, money and effort.

Your marriage is your long term investment where your dedication is required to increase its strength over a period of time. It requires a sacrifice of some present asset, such as time, money and effort.

We see many times people are more serious about their investment than their marriage which should be otherwise.

People take more time in analyzing which car to buy than to analyze about their own marriage.

In our society we see people don't think much or give a thought about their marriage. For them marriage is a one day grand affair with favorite honeymoon destination accompanied with lots of shopping, food and enjoyment. Actual marriage journey starts after honeymoon period is over about which no one thinks or gets themselves prepared.

Generally parents are also not so open about it and they only teach about adjustments in marriage. This is only for girls and for boys there is no guidance at all.

Have you ever heard a boy being told to adjust because after marriage he'll have to adjust with his wife?

Actually there is no proper guidance for girls and boys both before and after marriage. When things go out of hand after marriage there is no trend of getting help from the counselor who is better option than any family members who can't remain unbiased.

Including family members to resolve your personal conflict is the biggest mistake people make in their life. They unknowingly act as catalyst in ruining your relationship. You know even a best surgeon can't perform surgery of his own child. He takes him to the other surgeon. We need to understand this. If your marriage is going through a rough patch it is always better to consult a counselor for advice rather than involving your family members to make matter worse.

CHAPTER THREE

CASE 2

Nilesh and Nilima both were from very reputed and well off family. They both were successful in their respective careers and their marriage was solemnized by their parents. It was a big fat Indian marriage full of dazzle and glare followed by their favourite destination honeymoon. Their marriage remained talk of the town for many weeks. But after three months of marriage Nilima filed divorce case against Nilesh and they got separated.

Now here the question arises what could have gone so wrong in such a short time that they decided to take this step?

Nilima accused Nilesh for being a psychopath and an abusive husband and Nilesh accused Nilima of imprudent, delinquent and reckless behavior. As accusation from both the ends were very strong neither of the families tried for reconciliation and they got separated legally.

Just like their marriage their divorce also became talk of the town but no one exactly knew what happened.

Here are some of the points to consider---

Nilesh and Nilima both were living in a new city after marriage due to their jobs. After coming back from their honeymoon they both resumed their offices. Since they were living alone there was no one to help them out in their household chores. Though they had kept a maid for their help but still the house work load was too much for both the working partners.

Sometimes the maid would take leave without informing, leaving Nilima in helpless condition. Many times their breakfast would be missed; their dinners were irregular—in all no systematic order in food intake. Half of the time their house would be in total mess. Clothes, bags, food packets, sock all lying here and there. Nilesh didn't have the habit of putting things in their proper place and Nilima was getting exhausted out of limit. Slowly their arguments started getting converted to fights and abuses and sometimes Nilima would go to her friend's house for night stay.

Their sexual life was also getting affected and things started going out of their hands. They were not getting time to even discuss about this problem as during weekdays they were busy in their office and during weekends they would do other household chores like washing clothes, bringing groceries, fruits and vegetables and going out for dinner or to their friend's house.

Their relationship started to deteriorate at a fast pace and no effective measures were taken on time. This resulted into breaking of their marriage.

Man and woman both have their needs. Man has sexual needs more while woman has emotional and safety needs more. Safety needs include a hug, loving gestures, holding hands and all those things which can give her the feeling of security about her relationship.

When needs do not get satisfied it leads to frustration, anguishes and irritation. Unknowingly the person then starts losing his/ her temper on petty things.

Any relation especially of husband and wife takes time to develop, take roots and become strong. During initial period of marriage it is the responsibility of both husband and wife to take out time for their partners and spend quality time with them to understand them better.

In arrange marriage you know nothing about the other person --- what's their likes, dislikes, nature, behavior, wishes, expectations and many more. For this KT i.e., knowledge transfer, time is required. As I have said before marriage is a lifelong investment which requires your time, money and effort. Of the three assets time is prime important.

It is the primary responsibility of the husband to earn and take care of needs of the family just like the primary responsibility of the wife is to take care of her house and family. Though it sounds much outdated or orthodox, this is the universal truth.

This does not by any way means that husband should not do household chores to help their wife, of course they should but not at the cost of their primary responsibility. So also wife could also go out and do jobs but not at the cost of their primary responsibility.

There are many women doing jobs even after marriage, but they are fulfilling both their duties – office and home, very well. They have that much capacity and even support either internal or outside, to look after their work and family equally well. Internal support includes family members and outside support includes full time maid or helper. But if you don't have that much capacity and support why put your married life and your health at risk.

Calculation is very simple, full time jobs are of 9 hours and if it is from private sector then it conveniently gets increased to 10 to 11 hours. Including travelling time makes it 11 to12 hours. We need 8 hours of sleep in a day and combining this as well makes it almost 20 hours. Now we are left with only 4 hours to prepare food, complete all household chores and personal chores, do prayer, exercise, meditate, spend quality time with our partner, checking our social media and all such stuff.

There are many cases of women who wreck their health and happiness in their stubbornness to do jobs. In the absence of any strong support these women ends up getting no time for personal fitness, meditation and systematic intake of nutritious food. These result in deficiency of iron, calcium, vit. B, vit. D, zinc and many other vital nutrients. Constant work stress of house and office results in many ailments like blood pressure, diabetes, thyroid etc., which then leads to infertility or complications during pregnancy.

Sometimes we with our own hands create complications in our life.

What's this life with full of care

There's no time to stand and stare

Sometimes it is imperative to analyze about our life. What am I doing?

How am I doing?

What is my priority?

Am I really happy?

Am I living my life to the fullest?

Is this what I really want?

This self-introspection is very necessary for everyone.

"First impression is the last impression"

Though everyone know this, they forget to apply where its need is the most—in marriage.

The image that is developed initially about a person doesn't change so easily.

If a negative image is formed about a person that won't change into a positive one so easily and vice versa.

If a positive image has been developed in your subconscious mind about your spouse then however rough patch your relationship is going through and your mind will arouse you to end this relation but still your relationship will sail through because in the end it's the subconscious mind that makes the final verdict.

So this initial period of marriage is very crucial for the future of our relation and we have to be in our best mode on, because this is the time when our image is created in our partner's mind.

It is not imperative for a woman to leave her job after marriage but if she's feeling that things are not going smoothly then she should discuss this openly with her partner and take action/s accordingly. After all relation comes first and it should be given utmost importance.

Many marriages are short-lived because couples don't take proper decisions on time. They don't communicate their problems, discrepancies to the other. Communication gap and communication failure are causes of many problems that spur out in the relation.

CHAPTER FOUR

CASE 3

Nagma and Atif got married thirteen years ago. From the start itself their marriage was going through rough patch. Even their first night was ruined as their room was not prepared and they had to sleep with the other guests who came for their marriage. Atif's earning was very nominal so he had to depend on his mother's pension for his needs and wants. Atif's mother never liked Nagma and their relation was soured primarily due to her actions and Nagma's reactions.

Atif never took care of her or her needs. He barely talked to her and used to spend all his free time with his mother. Many times he would sleep in his mother's room leaving her alone. Feeling financially and socially paralyzed Nagma then decided to start working.

When Nagma got a job in different city coincidently Atif too got posted in other city.

He took his mother with him and Nagma took their son. As their relationship was never in its bloom state, this long distance made it wilt.

Nagma tried to reignite their relation by taking unpaid leaves from her office so that they can spend some time together as a family but here also she failed. Atif was living in an RK (room with kitchen) with his mother so when Nagma came to him she had to sleep in the kitchen. They were having no privacy, no personal talks, nothing. Many times Atif's mother would complain about Nagma to him causing their fights and even physical violence by Atif.

Nagma tried to convince him to move to a bigger house but Atif"s mother was adamant of not moving, rather she blurted out why Nagma wants so much privacy with her husband as they are not newly married. Atif was a blind follower of his mother use to do just as his mother says. He use to physically abuse and body shame her.

Gradually Nagma realized that her husband would never change for the better. So after thirteen years of sorrows, trouble, struggles, sacrifices and countless efforts she left him taking their son with her.

Though no divorce petition was filed still permanently they got separated. Atif never tried to save his marriage, neither before nor after separation. He and his mother convinced everyone in their family and society that it was all Nagma's fault by falsely accusing her of wrong doing.

Though Nagma was accused by the society for leaving her husband and breaking her own house, she and her family were happy of taking this decision.

Marriage is based on two important pillars- Love and Respect. Marriage is considered strong if it has both the element. Even one of the two can make it run though not so smoothly. But marriage can never survive if both the elements are absent

Nobody wants to stay in such a meaningless marriage where love and respect does not prevail.

Here Nagma was lucky to have a job and supportive parents. In many such cases woman decides not to leave marriage for the sake of their children. Many Indian women sacrifice their careers to run the house post marriage. Their years of labour go unrewarded if it ends in divorce with no claim left on matrimonial property. This little financial autonomy stops them from getting divorced. Many times men take advantage of this situation, they know that she has no place to go after marriage no matter how badly they treat her.

Don't marry someone if you don't need a partner in your life. Don't marry if you can't or don't want to take their responsibility. There are many people in our society who doesn't marry and remain single forever due to their own reasons. Ruining someone's life can never be justified with any amount of reasons you give. You can convince everyone but how will you convince God?

Remember, your Karma will definitely come back to you.

It is never the responsibility of a mother-in-law to take care of her daughter-in-law. When a boy marries a girl, she becomes his responsibility. Marriage is a lifelong contract between the two that-

They would take care of each other needs.

They would protect each other from all harm and danger.

They would respect each other.

Initially the responsibility of taking care of the partner is more on the husband because it's not he who has left his home and came to a new house with totally unknown people, different atmosphere, different customs and behaviors, different timetable and almost everything different. It is actually husband's responsibility to make his wife feel comfortable and included in his family. Let's understand this with another CASE.

Riya and Kunal got married 9 years ago. It was an arrange marriage and they were completely unknown to each other. During their marriage day itself Kunal's family members got annoyed with Riya's family over some arrangement issues. During Bidaai when none of his family members came forward to take the bride it was Kunal who took charge of the situation and he himself came forward to take Riya with him.

Kunal proved himself a true gentleman and a caring husband from the beginning itself. Back home at Kunal's native place where nobody use to ask Riya about what she wants or need, it was Kunal who was taking full care of all her needs. From morning tea to hot water for bath, from washing clothes to drying them, from lunches to dinner, Kunal was doing every bit to make Riya feel comfortable in his house. Though his family ignored her and deemed her insignificant and non-essential part of their family, it never affected Riya too much because Kunal was there to give her importance and take care of all her needs.

Even after nine years of marriage Riya does not feel included or part of Kunal's family nor her equation with them are so good, but still this did not caused any major trouble in their own marriage. Their marriage is strong enough to withstand any storm.

No marriage is perfect. Only when two people are ready to fulfill their duties and responsibilities towards each other only then marriage becomes perfect for them.

What do you think had Kunal also acted the same way as his family members from the start, had they been able to complete nine years happily?

Riya is not the only girl who is ill-treated and ignored by her in-laws due to some or the other reason. There are many girls in India who tolerate this silently. Life becomes unbearable when even her husband on whose trust she came to that house, does not give respect or pay heed to her needs. Some tolerate it and some brake through it but in both the cases marriage is compromised.

With great power comes great responsibility

Husband should understand that they enjoy higher status in their marriage because they have larger role to play. They have to keep balance between their maternal family and their newly formed family. When they fail in keeping balance then the problem arises. They should always keep in mind that their wife and mother will always have discrepancies, disputes, complains and discontent regarding each other. Ignoring these and remaining unbiased is what they should be doing but rather they get carried away by these complains and discontent and act hastily resulting to spurting of problems.

It is the duty of couples to protect the respect and honor of their partners. Remember if you say one thing against your partner your family will start saying fifty more things against them. Never give them the opportunity to do that. Whatever differences and grievances you have with your partner, try to solve them privately. Generally men get married between 27 to 33 years of age and women between 20 to 25 years. In this age a person is mature enough to solve their problems and handle it efficiently.

Many times people make their private life public by telling each and every issue regarding their partners to their family members. If you think by telling your issues to others will ease your situation- think once again.

People savor the disputes between husband and wife. Also, by telling your issues to them you are actually compromising your partner's respect and honor. After sometime your conflicts may get resolved but the impact it had on people whom you confided with will not be reversed.

By telling others, your issues with your partner, you have actually created a negative image of your partner in their mind. Once a negative image is created instantly the respect for that person diminishes and it is then reflected clearly in their behavior. Now you yourself have created a negative vibe between your family members and your spouse, resulting more spurting of problems.

There is a famous saying in Hindi ---

Miya Biwi ki Ladaai Dudh ki Malai

Means husband wife conflicts are like cream in the milk. If you boil the milk, the cream in it will instantly get melted into the milk.

Now if you put some drops of lemon juice in it, what will happen?

Milk will get cuddled.

Now by any mean can you make that cuddled milk back to its original form?

No!!

Including others in your personal matters is just like putting lemon juice in the milk. You'll then be unable to reverse the impact it will have on your relation.

In our Indian society, son-in-laws are given much importance. They are given more respect, more attention, more hospitality and everything more!!

In any caste, class or region this scenario remains same everywhere.

The status of a son-in-law is so high in the eyes of his in-laws that even if the girl confide with them about their issues or conflicts nothing major would happen. Here I'm not at all suggesting girls to do it, but even if she does they won't judge their son-in-law or form a negative image so easily, rather they would try to explain their own daughter—

You should adjust

Forgive and forget

These things happen in a marriage

Make his favorite dish and conciliate

You make the first move and say sorry

And so on.

But can this be other way round?

Would a mother tell her son to adjust with his wife, say sorry to her, conciliate and end the fight.

Hard to even imagine cause it's never this way.

Here we're talking about the general population. Exceptions are there and you'll find them in every field.

There are many people who do treat their daughters-in-law just like their own daughters. They give them respect, importance, take their advice, listen their views, include them in their family decision, guide them, help them, give them gifts, prepare their favorite dishes and many more.

But these types of people are very few in our society and generally majority of people especially mothers-in law are not so found of their daughters-in law.

CHAPTER FIVE

CASE 4

Reema got widowed at an early age. She didn't get much time to enjoy her married life. Her late husband was very loving and caring towards her and she had very beautiful memories of him. After his death Reema decided not to re-marry as she didn't wanted those blissful memories to fade. She decided to live the rest of her life taking care of her family. Her family was supportive to her and they respected her decision so they never pressurized her to re-marry.

Ramesh was a divorcee. His wife left him and his daughter, never to return. He then filed divorce case against her and started looking for someone to marry as he was unable to take care of his daughter and mother.

Ramesh met Reema through a middleperson and meeting her for the first time itself made him realized that she is the perfect match for him. Though Reema initially was humming and hawing over marriage, Ramesh convinced her by telling his miserable condition of not being able to look after his daughter. Taken away by her emotions she finally agreed to marry him.

Reema belonged to a rich and reputed family. She herself was a successful businesswoman and was financially stable. She married Ramesh with the sole purpose to experience the bliss of married life and motherhood. As she didn't had any child she accepted Rakesh's daughter as her own.

Reema expected Ramesh to be caring, understanding and be her best friend she could confide with, just like her late husband. Rakesh married Reema because he urgently needed someone to take care of his daughter and old mother. After just few months of their marriage, conflicts started erupting between them. Rakesh was very short-tempered fellow and he had the habit of making mountain of a molehill. Due to his this habit they were having constant fights and conflicts.

Rakesh's house was very small as compared to Reema's house and it was lacking in many facilities, most importantly privacy. It was so small that it couldn't even provide private space to the couple. Reema was facing much problems adjusting into that house plus the irritable behavior of Rakesh was making situation worse. Their troubled relation was affecting Reema's relation with Rakesh's daughter as well. She started staying away from Reema. All these situations were causing mental agony to her but she was helpless without solution.

Some people advised Reema to try for a baby. A baby can subsides their differences and re-ignite the love between them. So she decided to try this out as well, if at all it would make things better. She consulted a doctor regarding this and she asked her to come with her husband.

Many times Gynecologist do asks women to come along with their husband when they want to start a process or when things are complicated and needs attention. There can be many reasons to it.

But when Reema told her husband to come along with her to the doctor he accused Reema of doubting him to be deficient. He also blurted out that he is already a father while Reema couldn't become a mother, so it is she who should be tested and not he. As if this was not enough, he even called all his family members and told them that Reema is accusing him to be infertile.

After that situation got so difficult that she went back to her parents' house in a hope that may be Rakesh would realize his mistake and would come to take her home. But even after two months when there was no sign of improvement Reema decided to go back herself and start afresh.

Things didn't got better because communication failure or I would say communication disaster still persisted between them. Whatever one was saying the other was understanding it in a completely different manner. If Reema would call him to ask about his whereabouts out of concern, Rakesh would accuse her of keeping an eye on him every time. Their relation started going downhill and Ramesh started ignoring her to the extent that he wouldn't listen nor give attention to her.

This was the worst feeling that Reema was experiencing, she had to live with those people who were ignoring her to the extent that she was non-existent to them.

All these fights, conflicts and ignoring attitude of Ramesh were taking a toll on Reema's health. It was then that her family intervened and tried for patch up between them. But Ramesh was adamant that it's all her fault as she is short-tempered, non- adjusting and haughty. He has actually done a favor by marring their widowed daughter. Realizing that it's fruitless to talk with such a ruthless man, they took their daughter with them.

It's not hard to understand why this marriage didn't work. Ramesh showcases the characteristic of male chauvinism which was being aggravated by his family blind support. He neither had love nor respect for her. While Reema married because she needed a life partner Rakesh married her because he needed a care-taker for his daughter and mother. This image of a care-taker was so imprinted in his mind that he was unable to give wife's rights to her. So, though he knew it is his responsibility to take care of her needs and keep her happy, his sub-conscious mind was restraining him from doing so.

Here Reema took the wrong decision of marring someone much below her standards. Even after knowing that Ramesh has a very nominal income and his house is also very small, she took the decision of marring him, carried away by emotion. Marriage decision should not be made by emotions or for the sake of doing social-service. Adjustments are there in marriage but it also has its own limitations.

Only in reel life a princess can live happily with a poor guy but not in real life. Materialistic things also have their own importance. You cannot live your whole life in uncomfortability. Marriages can survive in caste difference but not class difference. Many teenager girls also do the same mistake drawing away in emotions and then their life becomes unbearable for them. It is the responsibility of every parent to guide their children regarding this topic.

Here the problem was not just about financial crunches and insufficient facility and privacy, but also male chauvinism which was rooted deeply within Rakesh. He never improved or changed for a better because he had unconditional support from his family. They had justifications for his every misconduct. As I have pointed earlier, people savor disputes between husband and wife.

Rakesh had the habit of making everything public and his family, in the pretext of solving his problems, was making things worse. No doubt his ex-wife must have left him due to the same reason.

From this case we also learned that before marrying a divorcee it is imperative to do a thorough investigation. If a person cannot carry on relationship with one partner, there is no guarantee s/he can carry on with other as well. Of course conditions apply.

According to a survey conducted by online matrimonial portal Jeevansathi.com, almost 70% of girls get married before they turn 25, which means either they get no time or very less time for their career formation. After marriage they're overly piled up with household responsibilities and bearing and rearing children, leaving them with no option to go out and work full time if they don't have any support.

These women find themselves financially broken if at all they get divorced or if they want to come out of their abusive and depressed married life because of two main reasons ---

Lack of experience to start their own career.

Lack of financial support from their parents due to various reasons.

As it is always a woman's life whose is at stake in marriage, it is their prime responsibility to look into each and every aspect consciously while deciding to marry. Surprisingly people make more analysis and take more time while buying a car than marrying someone.

One of the main reasons of divorces is the fact that we don't understand the true meaning of marriage. Every marriage in any caste is a lifelong commitment and a promise to each other.

In Hindu marriage seven vows are taken around the sacred fire by the couple

1. *To provide welfare and happiness in each other life*

2.

To protect each other through all phases of life

3.

To look after their children and being loyal to each other

4.

To express gratitude towards each other and be responsible parents to their children

5.

To become best friend and well-wisher of each other

6.

To fill each other heart with happiness

7.

To stay together for eternity

Marriages in every caste mean the same. It is actually the promises between the two. If couples understand the true meaning of marriage, then there will never be a divorce between them.

We often hear people associating marriage with adjustments, sacrifices, duties, responsibilities, patience, perseverance and many more heavy words. By connecting marriage with these words we're actually making it appear more difficult to ourselves and to the others. No doubt adjustments are there in marriage but with only adjustments marriage becomes compromised and compromised marriages are always weak, damaged and flawed.

CHAPTER SIX

CASE 5

Vaibhav and Jyotsna were married for four years. They were living together along with Vaibhav's mother. After four years disputes and fights between the two started taking place more often, so much so that they both then decided to end their marriage.

A very straightforward case of divorce but if we look closer we will see even after four years of marriage Jyotsna was not being able to conceive.

Like many mother-in-laws Jyotsna's mother-in-law also thought that she is infertile and now she started finding faults in everything that Jyotsna does. Their relation was not so good even before but now things were getting worse. Vaibhav's mother started complaining a lot about Jyotsna to him. Vaibhav who was already coming home tired from his office use to get infuriated and frustrated over these daily issues. As a result all his anger use to come down on Jyotsna and seeing this even Jyotsna's anger would come down on Vaibhav. Slowly their relationship got so ugly that they started raising hands on each other. Vaibhav's actions were mostly provoked and Jyotsna's actions were defensive and in retaliation.

Their relation started deteriorating in a fast pace and after sometime they decided to get separated instead of making each other's life hell.

After separation Vaibhav's mother started convincing everyone that it was all Jyotsna's fault as she was never a good wife. She uses to fight a lot with her husband on petty issues. It was them who were tolerating her from the beginning. Therefore they decided to dissolve this marriage before they both could harm each other.

It is not uncommon in our society to throw a woman out of her house if she is unable to bear a child. Earlier this process was open but now it is covered under the box of incompatibility.

Most of the time divorces due to this reason take place when the couples are living with their family. Many childless couples are still living happily and opting for adoption because they live away from their family.

This is actually a bitter reality of our society. In-laws never let their daughter-in-law live in peace if she is infertile.

No matter how much we are modern and open minded person when it comes to daughter-in-law we become orthodox and narrow minded.

Here also exceptions are there. Some people treat their daughter-in-law just like their own daughter and give them all the rightful freedom, love and care that they deserve. But such people are very few and could not outnumber those we studied before.

CHAPTER SEVEN

CASE 6

Sandhya was a second year B.Com student while Santosh was a 27 year old auto driver. They both met each other outside the college and then onwards started dating each other. Everyday Santosh used to take her to her college and bring her back to her house in his auto. They both felt attracted to each other and Sandhya in her adolescence was enjoying this adrenaline rush every time she saw him. One day Sandhya eloped with him and got married against her family's wishes.

After marriage things started getting difficult for Sandhya. Living in a small room with little amenities was something she didn't gave a thought before marring him. After few months Santosh developed drinking habit which worsens the situation. He used to physically assault and abuse her under the influence of alcohol.

Santosh and his family had many demands. They wanted bike, cash and gold from Sandhya's parents. When these demands were not fulfilled they started torturing Sandhya. Physical abuse, body shamming, character assassination became daily routine. After four years and two pregnancies later Sandhya finally left Santosh and filed for divorce and custody of her child.

Dowry harassment cases are not limited to a particular caste or economic class. It is found everywhere. Even now when dowry is a punishable offence it is still practiced in our society. Uttar Pradesh, Bihar and Tamil Nadu rank among the highest in taking dowry and therefore dowry harassment cases are reported more there.

In many other places dowry is taken in the form of "Gifts". Many times family of the groom doesn't demands gifts directly but they expect them and when these expectations are not fulfilled, problems start erupting between the bride and her in-laws. These problems slowly take the form of fights and abuses which then ends up with a legal separation.

CHAPTER EIGHT

WHAT WE LEARNED

1. Communication is a two edged sword. It can either make or mar your relation. What we wanted to say to our partner must be delivered clearly and after delivering, it should be checked whether they interpreted it in the same way in which we wanted them to. Any gap in communication can give rise to many misunderstandings and ill-feelings which in the long run ruin the matter.

Every couple, however busy they are, must take out time for each other. Spending quality time with the partner increases the intimacy between two and they get to know and understand each other well.

Even during fights or disputes communication should never be broken or stopped because it decreases the chances of rectification.

Things said at the right time have enormous positive impact and things said at the wrong time have enormous negative impact.

Generally people do this mistake of giving lectures and advices when their partner is ill or having some medical issue or condition. They immediately pour out their frustration on them not realizing the immense damage it can do to their relation. This should be avoided as things can be said anytime once they recover.

If your partner is ill then it is your duty and prime responsibility to take care of them and do the needful. By doing this you are not doing any favor on them rather fulfilling your responsibility.

2. When a couple plans a baby it is imperative for both of them to understand the challenges they would now be facing for many months to come and get themselves mentally prepared.

As it is a very long period, nine months before delivery and many months after that, mostly relation goes through rough time during this period. Woman already goes through a lot, mentally and physically, while bearing and rearing a child so it is the responsibility of a husband to give her physical and emotional support to her.

It is recommended that husband should get some information regarding pregnancy so that he understands what his wife is going through. Generally it is seen that men don't have any knowledge regarding this topic and thus act foolishly in critical times.

3. When you join a new job it requires more time and effort from your side so that you gain expertise and get used to it. Marriage is also a full time job with lifetime contract. During initial period it requires more effort and focus from both the partners, failing which causes many disputes and discrepancies.

It is therefore advisable for women to leave their job during initial period of marriage if they don't have any solid support to look after their household chores, because it becomes very straining to look after both of them. You can always get a new job may be even better than the previous if you have experience, but this is not in case of marriage.

Generally people give more importance to their jobs than marriage which actually should be otherwise. It is as if they consider getting a new partner is much easier than getting a new job. People are always seen ready to make any amount of sacrifices for their job but not for their marriage. This thinking causes rift between them.

I'm not saying don't give importance and attention to your job, of course you should as it is the sole method to earn your living and carry on with your responsibility especially for men, but be mentally prepared to give the same amount of importance to your marriage as well.

Very often we see that man moves out of his maternal house happily in search for a job or to join a new job but he resist doing so if his partner and family members are not bonding well or having trouble living together.

4. Privacy and private space are important aspect of married life. If you think you won't be able to provide or get private space with your partner its time you re-think about the marriage. Lack of privacy is the cause of many disputes to take a vicious form which otherwise could have got solved easily with mutual talk.

Physical abuses and domestic violence can never be justified with any amount of explanations given. It's actually shameful act and disgusting raising your hand on your partner.

Many times justification is given that she was speaking insolently with her husband so he raised his hand in anger. But if she was speaking insolently, you too can do the same, why use your hands when she is using her tongue. This is where "an eye for an eye" concept fits well.

Body shaming is the derogatory remarks on physical appearances. It weakens a relationship to its core. Make sure body shaming is avoided even in disputes and anger, because after sometime your anger may subside, your disputes may get resolved, but the words used for body shaming will always remain in the mind.

Women generally become victim of body shaming because their body changes a lot after marriage. Strenuous routine, bearing and rearing children, sleepless nights, in-laws stress and all these things take a toll on her health, physically and internally. So we see women are more susceptible to gaining weight after marriage then men. Here I'm not suggesting don't do anything about it, of course you should as much as you could.

After marriage physical appearances of your partner should never become a matter of concern for you. Do you ever judge your parents, siblings and other family members on the basis of your appearances, then why do so with your partner?

5. Do not involve any third person in your husband wife issues. Try to solve them mutually however complicated they may be. If you think even after trying, the issue is not resolving, take the help of a marriage counselor, but never, I repeat, NEVER EVER TAKE THE HELP OF YOUR FAMILY MEMBERS.

It ruins the chances of getting thing resolved.

Family members can never give unbiased opinion. It is very much obvious. Just like a surgeon can never perform surgery on his child however proficient s/he may be, so also family members can never give unbiased or just solutions however egalitarian, enlightened and fair they may be.

6. God creates life on the earth. He is the only one who can bless you with a child. No doubt today science has touched great height and it has developed many procedures due to which many childless couples have become parents successfully but still to make it successful is in God's hand. He is the only one who makes things possible. If you genuinely believe in God then why blame a woman for not being able to conceive?

Did you put any condition before marriage that if she could not become a mother then you'll leave her? If no, then hoe could you think of doing so with her.

In such situation, it is the duty of the husband to stand with her wife and protect her from the taunts of the family members and give her comfort and encouragement.

7. Dowry is a social evil in our society that has caused unimaginable tortures and crime towards women and polluted the Indian marital system. Now it's time that men stand against dowry system. Their conscious should not allow them to take money for marriage which is actually a nuptial bond with equal partnership.

His ego should be hurt thinking that he himself has put a price tag on him.

Dowry cannot be stopped completely with any amount of laws against it. It can only be eradicated when men will find it disgusting and will completely stand against it.

CHAPTER NINE

GENERAL CAUSES OF DIVORCES

In India, divorces are a big deal. And they are! It is painful process but sometimes that is necessary for survival. The impact of divorce is severe but it is much harder on women in our society.

It is seen that men recover faster from their wounds of divorces than women. It is easier for divorcee men to marry again than women. Mental trauma in women, before and after divorce is much more than men.

Our society had always looked down upon divorcee women and it is unanimously considered that divorces are due to faults and flaws of women. Men generally come out clean from this dirty procedure.

But now this biased thinking of the society is changing gradually and now even men are held equally responsible and accountable for breaking their marriage.

Now let's look into the causes of divorces.

1. A Traumatic Truth

One of the prime grounds for seeking divorce is abuse and trauma in the relationship. Abuse whether, physical, mental or emotional by men is an age old issue, but it is the rising awareness of rights, a better understanding of the law and growing independence of modern women, that is now taking these cases to the court.

Another factor to consider is that majority of the families now has two kids who are the apple of their eyes. They are raised with lots of love, care and attention. When these children face abuses, ignorance and belittlement after marriage they find it very hard or impossible to bear or tolerate such kind of behavior towards them. Even parents then cannot tolerate physical abuses on their daughters and they then themselves file the divorce case.

Physical violence on wife is generally a provoked action done under the influence of alcohol or empoisoning by the family.

According to reports, 31% of married women have reported to experience physical abuses by their spouses. But there are still many cases which do not come to light due to the woman's fear of being abandoned by her husband or being tortured more after reporting.

2. Changing Status of Women

In the last few decades, the status of Indian women has undergone a tectonic transformation. Women today are fiercely independent in terms of their finance, social status and mental strength. They are no more dependent on men in their life. In fact, today many women are earning more than their male counterparts.

This change in the status of women in a patriarchal society is resulting in ego clashes. In our society, taking care of the house and family is considered responsibility of a woman. Though there is nothing wrong as someone has to take care of them also and a woman is considered best in doing so. Things turn bad when while fulfilling the outside responsibilities, house and family are overlooked. This also results in fights, arguments and discrepancies between the couples and slowly their relationship starts to fall apart.

3. Equations With The In-Laws

In India, we live in a close-knit family that has its own set of rules, traditions and customs. More than 45% of Indian couples live with their parents and that comes with its own set of challenges. From over interference to adjusting to a restrictive setting to deprivation of privacy, many things can lead to clashes between the couples.

While it is true that family gives us strength and support, sometimes the family could become the root cause of divorce. It is the irony of our society where a man can leave his maternal house for a job but not to save his marriage.

Sometimes, because of the insecurity of losing control over their son or to have supremacy over the daughter-in-laws or insecurity of who will look after them in their old age, mother-in-laws deliberately creates rift between husband and wife.

Torture by the in-laws is not unheard and when husband don't take stand for his wife, relationship ends up with a divorce.

4. Marital Rape

Marital rape is a form of sexual violence which historically regarded as husband's right. Though in many places marital rape is defined as nonconsensual intercourse, it is actually the violence part in it which gives it a heinous look.

A woman experiences physical, mental and emotional trauma in marital rape and this leads her to end the marriage.

5. Adultery and Infidelity

Infidelity can be the most devastating thing that can happen to a relationship. In fact, according to a report infidelity is among the top 3 reasons why couples get divorced.

Adultery often refers to a physical relationship outside of marriage. It occurs when one partner is sexually involved with another without their partner's consent.

Infidelity is the act of being unfaithful to a committed partner. The criterion that defines infidelity can vary based on personal values, beliefs and expectations. As such, certain behavior or interactions may be acceptable to one couple but not to another.

Although infidelity and adultery are not same but similar, results of either one can lead to devastating betrayal of trust. Likewise both can cause irreparable damage to a relationship. An emotional affair can be as heartbreaking, if not more so, than a physical one, especially for women.

Earlier couples stayed in the relationship even after knowing about their partner's adultery because of social and family pressure. But today, they are finally acknowledging that it is better to live a single and happy life than to stay in a toxic, non-existent marriage that is smudged with adultery, infidelity and lies.

6. Broken Communication or

Communication Failure

Many modern marriages fail simply because partners aren't communicating well. While the stressful daily routine and straining work-life balance can take a toll, most of the time, communication fizzles out because of arguments and disagreements.

Communication failure also takes place because people are not good listener. They don't listen to understand but to answer back. This causes misunderstanding between them, when one person is saying something and the other person is interpreting it in a completely different way.

Time is conducive and every relationship needs its rightful amount of time to become strong. When this is not provided it fails drastically. Many times communication gap between the partners during the initial period of marriage also causes rift between them which if not filled on time can have a devastating effects afterwards.

Communication gap occurs when people don't convey their message clearly to the other person. It's the misinterpretation if information. In marriages communication gap occurs when couples don't state their wants or expectations directly to their partners. Beating around the bush is of no use if your partner does not understand your point.

7. Sexual Problems

The final nail in the coffin is the sexual issues in a marriage. Sex is a very important part of our life and sexual dissatisfaction can be frustrating. Having a strong sexual relationship nurtures the emotional and physical connection between the couple.

But with rising stress, worries and lack of routine of modern life, sexual problems are also on a constant rise. Impotency, loss of libido, erectile dysfunction, premature ejaculation and several such sexual issues can create trouble in paradise.

Generally a sexual problem in woman does not create so many problems in relation because she will anyhow co-operate with her partner either willingly or unwillingly. But sexual problems in man create much greater rift. It is the egoistic nature of man which makes him handle this situation in a most immature manner.

It is seen that many times man struggling with these problems deliberately creates problems with his wife to avoid physical intimacy. This in turn leads woman to grow suspicious about her husband. Slowly but surely sexual problems do leads to divorce if it is not discussed openly with the partner.

8. Dowry Harassment

In ancient times, the dowry was considered a woman's wealth because she had no claim on her natal family's real estate. In the late twentieth century throughout much of India, dowry payments have escalated and groom's parents sometimes insist on compensation for their son's higher education and even for his future earnings to which the bride will presumably have access. Many times higher amount is demanded by groom's family because it will then be used for giving dowry for groom's sister's marriage.

Dowry is a social evil and it has broken many marriages and financial stability of many parents. Many women face humiliation, taunting, abuses, harassments and even physical and mental tortures due to dowry. Some try to stand against it while many still tolerate it silently. Marriages constructed on heavy dowry are often fragile and frail and are susceptible to crumple. In the year 2020, 10366 cases were registered under the Dowry Prohibition Act while 7000 dowry death cases were reported in India. These are the registered figures analysis says more than 35% women face humiliation due to dowry.

9. Outdated Frame Of Mind

Earlier woman was considered inferior to man and daughter-in-laws were treated like second class citizens, with no rights, privileges, respect or admiration. But now society has changed, their mindset has also changed. Today women walk shoulder to shoulder with men. There is no field left where women have not proved their excellence. Family, education institutes, workplace, everywhere women are getting same opportunities and respect as men.

Problem arises when woman does not find this same mindset in her in-laws place. Putting on "ghungat", eating after everyone has done, not to speak your opinion, doing nothing unless taken permission, not going out alone are some of the many things still prevalent in many houses. They still consider it as an act of honor.

Biased thinking also creates trouble in a family, when thinking regarding their daughters and daughter-in-laws has a large disparity. Like, if the daughter's husband is taking care of her then he is a good husband, but if the son is doing the same, he instantly becomes a henpecked husband.

If the daughter's husband is taking her to a vacation then, it's her right, she deserves it, but if the son is doing the same thing then—

Why waste so much money and after that it will be marked as a huge favor done on the daughter-in-law by her husband and her in-laws.

All these biased thinking and attitude create rifts not only with in-laws but also between husband and wife. These attitudes directly hurt to the core and the genuine respect, love and concern for the in-laws fade away.

Now when both the parties are having ill-feelings for each other, it becomes difficult living under one roof and when husband doesn't agree on moving out, woman walks out alone.

10. Impulse Wedding

There are many cases where teenagers get married without considering the caste and class differences and after sometimes they end up with a divorce. There are so many cases where girls elope and marry with people below their status and when love subsides and reality sink in they come back crying to their parents.

Many times girls become pregnant in there illicit relationships which results in their forceful marriage. Mostly these marriages also do not last long.

There are few cases where couples meeting each other through a dating app get married without actually knowing each other or about their family background. Later on when they discover each other to be entirely different, they then decide to choose their unique paths with consented divorce.

11. Asexuality or Homosexuality

Asexuality is the lack of sexual attraction towards other or low or absent interest in or desire for sexual activity. It may be considered a sexual orientation or the lack thereof. People with asexuality have no true desire or need to engage in sexual or non-sexual activity like cuddling, hand-holding, etc.

Homosexuality is romantic attraction or sexual behavior between members of the same sex or gender. Both these sexual orientation plays havoc in married life. As asexuality and homosexuality are condemned or deemed disgraceful by the society, many people with this sexual orientation still get themselves married due to the pressure from the family or to save their honor in the society. Though they do get married but they remain in frustration and guilt which hampers them from leading a happy life with their partners.

Asexuality is many times not realized by a person. Means an asexual person may think that s/he is normal though s/he is not. This lack of realization creates more problems because here the person, not realizing their non-credibility, assumes their partners to be wrong i.e. over expecting or over demanding.

In short both these sexual orientation ultimately cause disputes, dissatisfactions, and ill-feelings for their partners which ultimately ends with a divorce.

CHAPTER TEN

9 GOLDEN MANTRAS

Divorces are not the end of the world

But it certainly makes life grey after it.

It is true that divorces are mentally and emotionally draining not just for the couples but also for their families. And if children are involved, divorces can be more difficult. It is therefore that we start our newly married life in a correct manner and maintain it accordingly.

One of the best ways to have healthy relation with your partner is to make him/her your best friend and treat him/her accordingly.

How do we treat our best friend?

1. Always Talk With Them

Either passed out of the college, doing job somewhere else, got married, having busy life or whatever the situation may be, we never stop talking to them. Somehow we do take out time from our busy schedule and talk our heart out to them. Either once in a week or two, we do take out time for them. So you see we do follow a routine without fail.

Simply we have to apply this rule on our partner. Talk to them. Never stop your communication as it leads to misunderstandings and prejudices.

Follow routine. Even if you both are too busy in your work decide time to talk, either during teatime or after dinner whichever suits you and try to follow that routine without fail.

Remember, many great wars have been averted through mutual conversation.

2. Protect Their Honor

We never let anyone hurt or make fun of our best friend. If someone tries to do so, we answer them back on behalf of our best friend.

This same rule is applicable on our partner as well. It is our responsibility to protect their honor especially in our own family. If someone is trying to humiliate them or insult them it is your responsibility to take a stand and defend them.

Husband and wife are two people with one soul; therefore they are also called better halves. So when someone tries to degrade your partner, it means they are degrading you.

The moment couple understands this fact many things can get resolved on its own.

3. Know Them

We all know our best friend very well. Their likes, dislikes, favorites, their usual behavior, their replies etc. We know almost everything about them and thus we do things accordingly.

This same rule is applied to our partner. We should know our partner so well that no words should be required to understand their mood, their feelings, their wants and needs. We should be able to understand on our own, what they'll say or ask and many more.

By knowing each other so well we complement each other and make each other complete. At this point our marriage reaches a new level of relationship.

4. Have Fun

We enjoy spending time with our best friend because it's so much fun. We laugh, joke tease, go out, eat, shop and party with them. It's not that we and our best friend are same, as everyone is unique and even twins can't have same thoughts and likes.

Fact is, we enjoy spending time and doing things together with our best friend.

Similarly, we should also enjoy spending time and doing things together with our partner. It should never be only what you like, what they like should also be important to you.

Happiness lies in making our loved one happy.

If they like shopping and you don't, sometimes do it for their sake. If they like eating out and you don't, sometimes do it for their sake.

Sometimes do thing what they like, sometimes what you like and many times what you both like. This helps to maintain balance in life.

5. Accept Them

Do we ever leave our best friend because they are too tall or short or too dark or fair? We look at them beyond these physical appearances. We accept them as they are, with all their flaws and strengths.

This must be our attitude for our partner also. After marriage their physical appearance should never become your concern. Any jokes, taunts, or comments on physical appearances should always be avoided because it hurts badly and they may feel offended. Body shamming is a complete NO even during fights and disputes.

Every person has some good and bad qualities. Nobody is perfect. When we marry a person it means we are accepting them with all their flaws and strengths.

Either short tempered or bore, less efficient in cooking or more, you have to deal with them accordingly. You can't say s/he is this this... so I don't like her/him. Accept their flaws and weaknesses and try to manage with them accordingly.

6. Exchange Gifts

We do give gifts to our best friend on special occasions or whenever we meet. Giving gifts in any relation is an important aspect as it strengthens our relation with them. Though we say, "What was the need", "We don't expect gifts from you", but actually we do feel ecstatic while receiving it. We do feel happy giving and receiving gifts.

This same principle must be applied in our married life as well. Giving gifts to our partners on special occasions make those occasions even more special. It creates intimacy between the two and helps create that much needed spark in our life. Every one like surprises and gifts even if they say they don't want or need.

In marriages, surprises and gifts do hold a special place and this should be remembered by all the couples.

7. Help Them

We are always ready to help our best friend. Whether their personal problems or some of their task to be done, if we could help them, we definitely help them.

This same rule must be applied in our married life. Always try to help them whenever they need. Solve their problems even if they don't ask for it. Share their work load even if that looks too small or insignificant, do it, because it does make a difference.

Massaging their head, giving them water, helping them in their household and personal chores, all these are very small things and doesn't requires much effort, but its impact is great. Slowly but surely all these little efforts strengthen the relationship between the couples.

8. Best Friend Forever

BFF!!! We not only just say it but also prove it correct. During our lifetime journey we make and leave many friends but that one friend remains with us forever, throughout our life. It gets embedded in our mind and soul, not to leave that friend at any point of our life.

This concept goes well with your marriage also. Marriages are forever. It's a fulltime and lifetime contract. It's a nuptial bond not meant to be broken. Once a partner, always a partner. Make sure to make your partner your BFF.

9. Be a Good Listener

Best friend is that one person with whom we confide all our problems, issues, concerns and whatever that is bothering us, knowing very well that, that information will never get leaked. We trust them and they lives up to our trust. They listen to us patiently. They always have time for us, ears for us. Whether they can solve it or not, do anything about it or not, they listen to us and give that much needed console.

This same principle must be applied in our marriage. Always be a good listener to your partner. Encourage them to tell you what's bothering them. Tell them that they can trust you and never break that trust. Be patient while listening and let them pour out all that is going in their mind. Never interrupt in the middle. When we share our problems with each other it deepens the bond between us.

NOTE: There might have been some repetitions of points here and there, but, I have done it purposely to stress those points in your mind.

Quotes

Marriage is like a garden

With rightful amount of

Water, sunlight and efforts

It yields surplus amount of

Flowers and fruits

Otherwise it gets converted

To a barren land.

Zarreen khan

I love being married

It's so great to find

That one special

Person you want to

Annoy for the

Rest of your life.

Rita rudner

A good marriage

Isn't something you find,

it's something you make

and you have to

keep on making it.

Marriage is not

About the wedding.

It's about the years

Of growing together

As individuals

And not giving up

On each other.

A divorce is like

an amputation: you

survive it, but there's

less of you.

Margaret atwood

People do not get Married planning to Divorce.

Divorce is the result

Of lack of preparation

For marriage and the

Failure to learn the

Skills of working together

As teammates in an

Intimate relationship.

Gary chapman

9 798887 494098

Printed by Libri Plureos GmbH in Hamburg,
Germany